SCHIRMER'S LIBRARY
OF MUSICAL CLASSICS

SEBASTIAN LEE

Op. 31

Forty Melodic and Progressive Études

For Violoncello

Edited and Fingered by

LEO SCHULZ

Book I contains a Biographical Sketch of the Composer by

RICHARD ALDRICH

IN TWO BOOKS

Book I (Nos. 1-22) — Library Vol. 639
Book II (Nos. 23-40) — Library Vol. 640

ISBN 978-0-7935-4871-2

G. SCHIRMER, Inc.

DISTRIBUTED BY

HAL•LEONARD®
CORPORATION

7777 W. BLUEMOUND RD. P.O. BOX 13819 MILWAUKEE, WI 53213

Forty
Melodic and Progressive Études.

⊓ Down-bow.
V Up-bow.

SEBASTIAN LEE. Op. 31, Book 2.

23. Exercise on the Cantabile.

Printed in the U.S.A. by G. Schirmer, Inc.

24. Exercise in Double-stops.

Piu mosso.

25. Exercise on the Staccato.

26. Exercise in different Bowings.

27. Exercise on different Arpeggios.

Allegro non troppo.

cresc.

f

G-string   A-string

p

28. Exercise for the Use of the Thumb.

Allegretto.

10

29. Exercise in the Broad Style of Bowing.

30. Exercise on the Appoggiatura and the Turn.

Allegretto grazioso.

31. Various Bowings.

Allegro non troppo.

32. Exercise in Flexibility, for the Right Wrist.

Moderato assai.

33. Characteristic Exercise.

Allegro risoluto.

34. Characteristic Exercise.

Allegro agitato.

G-string

D-string

15660

35. Trill-Exercise.

36. Exercise for giving elasticity to the wrist.

37. Exercise on the Light Staccato.

Allegro moderato.

(middle of the bow.)

38. Exercise in Double-stops.

Andante moderato.

espressivo

39. Chromatic Exercise.

Allegro non troppo.

40. Octave-Exercise.

Allegro brillante.

Fine.